Conducting a Telephone Interview

Master the art of conducting a telephone interview to make
the most effective hiring decisions

Vaibhav Gupta

Impackt Publishing
We Mean Business

Conducting a Telephone Interview

First published: September 2014

Production reference: 1230914

Published by Impackt Publishing Ltd.
Livery Place
35 Livery Street
Birmingham B3 2PB, UK.

ISBN 978-1-78300-036-4

www.Impacktpub.com

Cover image by Jarek Blaminsky (milak6@wp.pl)

Credits

Author
Vaibhav Gupta

Reviewers
Jason Carson
Iris Tianren Shen

Acquisition Editor
Nick Falkowski

Copy Editors
Tanvi Bhatt
Paul Hindle
Faisal Siddiqui

Project Coordinator
Venitha Cutinho

Proofreaders
Simran Bhogal
Paul Hindle

Graphics
Valentina D'silva
Abhinash Sahu

Production Coordinator
Adonia Jones

Cover Work
Melwyn D'sa

About the Author

Vaibhav Gupta is the founder and owner of the blog www.howtocrackaninterview.com. After his Master's degree in Business Administration from Leeds Business School, United Kingdom, his entrepreneurial spirit inspired him to start Oxygen Consultancy Services, a New-Delhi-based executive search and recruitment firm. The firm has been recruiting for global Banking, Insurance, Automotive, FMCG, Accounting, Research, and Business Consulting organizations including HDFC Bank, ICICI Prudential Life Insurance Company, Kotak Mahindra Bank, Nestle India Ltd., The Smart Cube India Pvt. Ltd., GE Business India Services, and KPMG. The firm has been extremely instrumental in hiring across all levels and business verticals.

Vaibhav has personally managed more than 10,000 interview cases in a period of 10 years and has also been a part of campus placement teams with many companies such as ICICI Prudential Life Insurance.

He is also a visiting faculty member at prestigious institutions such as Institute of Chartered Accountants of India (ICAI).

To provide comprehensive online information on the interview process and its basic nuances, he started the blog www.howtocrackaninterview.com, in which he has tried to provide an extremely broad and detailed spectrum of information regarding the interview process through highly interactive videos.

He has also authored *Job Winning Answers – Best answers to 105 trickiest interview questions*.

Acknowledgments

My book *Conducting a Telephone Interview* has not been created solely by me. There are a large number of people who have contributed directly or indirectly towards the making of this book. This book would not be complete without acknowledging those who have devoted their time and effort during the making of this book.

The biggest contributors are those 800 employees from various organizations across the globe who participated in my survey regarding telephone interviews and provided their honest feedback which provided the authenticity to my experience and interpretations. I would also like to thank my clients who I have worked with as a recruitment consultant over the last 10 years and who have been the greatest sources of my learning and experience in the field of hiring and interviews.

I would also like to thank Mr. Jason Carson—Director of Labour Relations/Human Resources and Safety at Brilion Iron Works, United States, profusely, as he supported my theories and clarified my doubts through his invaluable input. Despite being extremely busy, the enthusiasm and promptness with which he provided detailed answers to questions that I asked is commendable.

I cannot forget to thank P. Harihar—Senior Engineer, ARM, United Kingdom, who shared his experience of the telephone interview process and provided strength to the concepts and their advantages that are advocated in this book.

I would like to dedicate this book to my wife, Dr. Reena Gupta, and our beloved son, Maulik, who supported me in the greatest possible manner by being extremely understanding while I was juggling my time between carrying out my regular job and writing this book.

Everything I am capable of doing today is because of the world class education that my parents, Mrs. Neera Gupta and Mr. Anil Kumar Gupta, have provided to me using all possible means available to them, and I thank them from the bottom of my heart.

Finally, I would like to thank the publisher, Impackt Publishing, and their team of coordinators and editors for providing me with a great opportunity to write this book, showing faith in the content that I provided, and providing tips to refine the language of the book in order to make it a worthwhile reading experience.

About the Reviewers

Jason Carson has over 20 years of progressive human resource experience. Mr. Carson has worked for companies such as Walgreens, McDonalds Corp, Oshkosh Corp, Masco Corp, and currently works for Appvion in Appleton, WI. Mr. Carson is a business executive with proven ability to help design programs and create solutions that are both bottom-line-oriented and focused on long term success. This includes a strong focus on financial performance, operational success, and alignment of crucial talent to key linchpin positions. He has experience in both startups and turn-around opportunities, specializing in leading change throughout an organization.

Iris Tianren Shen is a Talent Sourcing Specialist working for Randstad Technologies, headhunting the most talented IT and financial professionals everyday for Fortune 500 companies. She started her career as a Career Assistant and realized her true passion was in talent acquisition, career planning, and HR consulting. She has guided hundreds of professionals with active listening, career advice, and new opportunity exploration.

Born in mainland China, Iris graduated from the University of Toronto with a Psychology degree, and has paved her recruiting career path with intrinsic interests, persistence, and faith in Canada. In her spare time, Iris devotes her efforts to volunteering to help children with autism and people in need.

Contents

Preface   **1**

Chapter 1: The Telephone Interview and Its Role in Hiring   **5**

Past and present times   7
   Recruitment scenario – pre-2008   7
   Recruitment scenario – post-2008   9
Telephone interviews – the key to saving time, effort, and money   10
Developing prospects is essential   13
Summary   14

Chapter 2: Are You Doing It Correctly?   **15**

Case study   16
Did you plan ahead?   17
Check your telephone etiquette   18
   Be sensitive   19
   Be cordial   19
   Be attentive   19
   Be natural   19
   Be distinct   20
   Be expressive   20
How well did you listen?   20
   Prepare adequately   21
   Avoid distractions   21
   Demonstrate genuine interest   22
   Ask open-ended questions   22
   Never jump to conclusions   22
   Assess regularly   22
Did you record it?   23
   Record the conversation   24
   Candidate assessment checklist   24
Did you sell the job?   24
The reform   25
Summary   26

Chapter 3: Plan, Conduct, and Assess   27

How to plan a telephone interview   28
  Macro-planning   28
    Purpose behind the hiring   29
    Expectations from the candidate   29
    The Tolstoy Trap   29
  Micro-planning   30
    Scheduling the interview   30
    Keeping all the documents ready   30
    Preparing your list of questions   30
How to conduct a successful telephonic interview   31
  Open-ended questions   32
    Work-related questions   32
    Candidate-centric questions   32
    Questions about the new job and organization   33
    The candidate's vision   33
    Behavioral questions   33
  How to be a lie detector   33
How to do a candidate assessment   34
  Academic excellence   35
  Profile relevance   35
  Market and industry knowledge   35
  Business knowledge and understanding of the job profile   35
  Personality traits   35
  Behavior and culture   35
How to sell the job   36
  Give a fair idea of the company's vision   37
  Future prospects and career development opportunities   37
Summary   38

Chapter 4: Avoid Common Mistakes   39

Planning phase   41
  One-sided scheduling of interviews   41
  Not analyzing and defining the requirement   41
  Unstructured interview   41
Communication errors   42
  Ambiguous role descriptions   42
  Not making the candidate comfortable   44
  Making the interview a monologue   44
  Using local slang, idioms, or dialect   44
Interview phase   44
  Testing knowledge and not action   45
  Not digging deep enough   45
  Trying to dodge the interviewee's queries   45
  Trying to make a mental note of most of the information   45

Assessment phase   46
   Intuition-based assessment   46
   Stuck in the Tolstoy Trap   46
   Using the wrong benchmarks for comparison   46
The job selling phase   47
Summary   48

Chapter 5: Master the Skill – Training and Development   49

Classroom training   51
Implementation   51
Summary   53

Preface

In 1876, Alexander Graham Bell patented one of the most revolutionary inventions the world has ever seen: the telephone. It was a device that transmitted voice through electrical signals through wires. A tribute to human ingenuity, within decades the telephone possessed the power to alter the concept of global communications. While brilliant engineers are rightly credited for the creation of great technological advancements, we should not forget that dynamic business managers are owed acclaim for their commercial expansion. After more than a century of global commercial development, the **telephone interview** is the modern heir of Bell's first famous telephone call to summon his assistant to his work room.

The telephone interview, though just a speck on the global communications sphere, is worthy of careful consideration as an important skill with a specific purpose. Getting it right can make all the difference to your business. Although some employers have been using the telephone as a precursor to face-to-face interviews for decades, the world is changing. Interviewing remotely has never before been given the prominence that it enjoys today, especially since the most recent global economic downturn in 2008.

These tumultuous times have forced all hiring managers to appreciate the importance of searching for and hiring global talent through the most cost-effective means available. It has also differentiated the top performers from the average candidates. Money alone won't attract top talent; one needs to offer more to lure the best employees. This has led to the amalgamation of hiring and sales processes.

This book focuses on creating a holistic approach to the telephone interview as an effective and cost-saving hiring strategy. Over five chapters, we'll cover the best ways to make the most of interviewing by telephone.

What this book covers

Chapter 1, The Telephone Interview and Its Role in Hiring, explains why you should include telephonic interviews as a key part of your hiring process, and analyzes and explains the benefits and savings they can potentially deliver. The chapter will show you how the telephone interview, if planned and conducted properly, can bring a strong positive impact on an organization's employee strategy.

Chapter 2, Are You Doing It Correctly?, gives you the capability to review and examine how you conduct telephone interviews currently as a basis for improving. As you read this chapter, it will encourage you to self-assess your current preparation process for telephonic interviews. It will help you set benchmarks that will act as comparison and measurement tools.

Chapter 3, Plan, Conduct, and Assess, will cover organizing an assessment strategy that has been designed to facilitate the hiring of the most competent candidate with the minimum financial outlay. Do you want to select the most competent candidate with minimum resources outlay? Optimizing each process and minimizing the risks in order to achieve the business objectives is what every manager aims at. Every recruiter wants to hire the best available candidate for a vacant job role. But hiring the best needs "planning". This chapter takes you through the essentials of planning—both on a micro and macro scale—and provides you with the necessary tools you need to conduct a highly optimized telephone interview process.

Chapter 4, Avoid Common Mistakes, lists all the commonly made mistakes a recruiter can make at any of the stages provided in the previous chapter and provides solutions and advice on how to avoid or fix them. "Trial and error" isn't a bad technique to understand the mistakes and correct them in many aspects of life and business. In some cases, it is almost considered essential, but recruitment doesn't belong to this theory. So it will be much better if recruiters can learn from the mistakes others made and avoid repeating them. Managing a bad hire can be the most harrowing experience for an organization. Therefore it's better to prepare an error-free telephonic recruiting environment.

Chapter 5, Master the Skill – Training and Development, concludes the book by showing you how to include telephonic interview skills development training in your regular training calendar to maintain competency. It also teaches you how to win support for the adoption of a wider training program related to telephone interviews from the key management team, which is essential for improving on a company-wide level.

What you need for this book

You should have a desire to enhance the productivity of the recruitment process, and accept that a restructuring of existing recruitment strategy is potentially required. Such restructuring must emphasize adopting and mandating processes like telephone interviews. Adopting it wholeheartedly would require the company to give equal weight to each step involved and examine existing processes critically in the light of the solutions advised in this book.

Who this book is for

If you are a recruiter, manager, leader, or anyone aiming to work in one of these situations, this is the book for you. Organizations run and perform because of their talented pool of resources. Efficiency of a process is directly proportional to the quality of employee who is running or managing it. Computers don't run organizations—people run computers, which in turn run organizations. Any professional person who understands this fact and wants to champion the tricky business of recruitment, especially over the telephone, would benefit from reading this book. Any leader who wants to hire the best employees at an optimized cost must read this book.

Conventions

In this book, you will find a number of styles of text that distinguish between different kinds of information. Here are some examples of these styles, along with an explanation of their meaning.

New terms and **important words** are shown in bold.

Make a Note

Warnings or important notes appear in a box like this.

Action Point

Action points appear like this

Reader feedback

Feedback from our readers is always welcome. Let us know what you think about this book—what you liked or may have disliked. Reader feedback is important for us to develop titles that you really get the most out of.

To send us general feedback, simply send an e-mail to `feedback@impacktpub.com`, and mention the book title via the subject of your message.

If there is a book that you need and would like to see us publish, please send us a note via the **Submit Idea** form on `https://www.impacktpub.com/#!/bookidea`.

Piracy

Piracy of copyright material on the Internet is an ongoing problem across all media. At Packt, we take the protection of our copyright and licenses very seriously. If you come across any illegal copies of our works, in any form, on the Internet, please provide us with the location address or website name immediately so that we can pursue a remedy.

Please contact us at `copyright@impacktpub.com` with a link to the suspected pirated material.

We appreciate your help in protecting our authors, and our ability to bring you valuable content.

>1

The Telephone Interview and Its Role in Hiring

What created the need for telephone interviews? After all, everything was running just fine without them. Or was it? How is it different from a traditional job interview process? Professionals understand that a job interview is a process of evaluating a prospective job candidate by the recruiter with the intention of exploring whether the candidate is suitable for the job in their organization or not. Now, it would be easy to assume that this interview process, when it happens via telephone, would be known as a telephone interview; this is only partially correct. A telephone interview never replaces a face-to-face interview, but is in fact a preliminary step to qualify the applicant for a detailed face-to-face interview.

As an experienced recruiter, I have seen the status of the telephone interview undergo a transition over the past ten years. It started with the candidates demanding a telephone interview because they wanted to make sure that they were being called for the right role, and not just to fill in the recruiters' monthly interview targets. It used to be a tug of war where the candidate wanted a telephone interview, while the recruiter wanted to interview the candidate face to face. Things changed over time and now the recruiter prefers to interview a candidate by telephone for the first round. The tug of war ended and candidates were no longer complaining. Yet, I observed that in most cases, telephone interviews were still strictly limited to the evaluation of basic communication skills and role suitability of the candidate.

The recession in 2008 altered the scenario entirely. The telephone interview gained prime preference for the recruiter as well as the interview candidate. Telephone interviews were no longer merely a means of basic screening. On parsing the interview data of 60 clients associated with my firm for the financial year 2010-2011, I can say that telephone interviews became a deciding factor in more than 80 percent of interview cases.

In this chapter, we will analyze how times have changed in the last ten years and the impact of these changes on candidates' attitudes and on recruiters' hiring strategies. We will also explore the key advantages a telephone interview delivers to a firm, as well as the candidate. A good telephone-interview process saves time, effort, and money for both parties.

This chapter highlights the reasons to develop prospective talent resources for organizations in the light of changing times, and demonstrates how to make telephone interviews an instrumental process in accomplishing this goal. You'll learn when, how, and why telephone interview gained the importance it enjoys today, and why that's important for your own hiring strategy.

Past and present times

The economic slump of 2008 changed many existing management theories, beliefs, concepts, and practices. My classification of past and present times could just as well be termed "pre-2008" and "post-2008". Let's review how recruitment scenarios changed before and after 2008.

"Before 2008, I used to get a large number of interview invitations from different hardware development companies for various positions available. But nothing really caught my interest," recalls P. Harihar, a senior engineer at UK-based global IT hardware organization ARM. *"But it was in 2010, when my present employer ARM UK offered me something that I was really looking for, and I shifted my base from Bangalore, India, to Cambridge, UK."* Harihar's story, shared with me after he had been interviewed for his new role first by phone, then twice in person, is far from unique. The change from blanket interviews to a specific, targeted process of matching Harihar's skills and needs and those of his company in the wake of the recession was conspicuous. And it made all the difference.

Recruitment scenario – pre-2008

Let's assume that "Company A" has targeted a **Compound Annual Growth Rate (CAGR)** of 35 percent for the next three years. In order to achieve this, an additional 200 professionals must be hired per quarter. The interview to hire ratio is 8:1, which means that 1600 candidates must be interviewed in a quarter to achieve the hiring target of 200 employees. Imagine that the number of working days in a quarter are 66, this would call for approximately 26 face-to-face interviews a day.

For some sectors such as IT/ITES, real estate, telecoms, banking, financial services, and insurance, the number of interviews organized per day increased five fold during the peak of their hiring before 2008, and companies seldom if ever held preliminary telephone interviews.

There were several reasons behind such gigantic hiring targets:

> ➤ The economic boom had provided a great opportunity for profit-oriented organizations to boost their businesses tremendously

> ➤ These organizations' prime focus was on enhancing business by adding a large number of customers to the existing portfolio, which in turn meant deploying larger staff

> ➤ Companies had the resources to plough into large hiring budgets

> ➤ Management was often more focused on quantity over quality

> ➤ As hiring was not an issue, firing was not a problem either, and high employee turnover was of little concern

> ➤ Since the job market offered ample opportunities, candidates were open to experimentation

> ➤ The job applicant's main attention was on a better compensation package, at least in the majority of cases

The results of all of this defined the hiring environment:

> ➤ No preliminary screening process existed, except resume vetting

> ➤ Interviews were more a case of trial and error rather than a well-defined process with a result-oriented approach, except for top leadership positions

> ➤ Essentially, in profit-oriented industries, corporate recruiters' primary concern was to arrange interview candidates to fill their targets, even if that meant compromising on the quality of the candidate, and agency recruiters complied with their clients' demands

> ➤ Most candidates never gave weight to role clarity; even if some did, they were convinced by the recruiters or the agents to attend the face-to-face interview

> ➤ There was a very low stick ratio; with job hopping being a common trend, the company that offered more money got the candidate, even if that meant resigning from the previous job in just six months

That was a common picture of recruitment for the majority of industries globally. However, many from both sides of the process began to understand that recruitment and job change respectively were the kind of decisions that must be taken more consciously. Those were the people who highlighted the need for telephone interviews.

Initially, telephone interviews were seen simply as an initial screening process. This had its own drawbacks:

> ➤ Recruiters did it primarily to carry out the initial screening of the candidate, which included verifying the facts given on the resume and evaluating their basic communication skills. This still left everything but the most basic evaluation to the face-to-face interview.

> ➤ Candidates primarily used it as a tool for assessing the kind of money offered in the role. Though some also used it to glean whether the role really suited them, or if recruiters were merely lining up candidates in order to meet their targets, the information exchanged remained cursory.

Undoubtedly, these screening interviews cut down on time and effort for the recruiter while improving the quality of candidates coming in, but only marginally. It turned out to be productive for the candidates as well, as now they had to attend fewer interviews in a job market full of prospects. Still, no one realized the true potential a telephone interview could offer.

Then, in 2008, the bubble burst and the recession changed everything.

Recruitment scenario – post-2008

The year 2008 began with global economic meltdown, critically affecting even the strongest of nations and organizations. Forget competition, companies were merely trying to keep themselves afloat in such turbulent waters. Even the most stable and employee-driven organizations were forced to issue pink slips to their most loyal employees. Worse were the humiliating ways in which such layoffs were carried out within the organizations that completely crushed the loyalty and feelings of security amongst those who stayed. During the hiring freeze (which lasted almost until 2010), organizations had ample time to redefine their processes. It was a time for introspection and learning. Every strategic move must now navigate the new waters of cost cutting, effectiveness, and productivity, leading to the scrutiny of each and every business process to achieve these goals. It also gave time to candidates to develop a holistic approach towards the process of a job search.

Some major changes emerged in organizational strategies and goals:

> The biggest challenge for companies became business retention

> Value business was given priority over numbers, which created the need for smaller teams of highly-effective performers

> Employers had faced the losses of bad hires, as well as the hammering of their face value in the employment market due to layoffs; hence, many became extremely vigilant of the recruitment process

> Cost efficiency became the prime target of every process, which created the need for stringent hiring methods

> Talent management and talent retention became the core focus of human resource strategies

Perhaps the biggest mutation was the way in which job opportunities were perceived by the applicants. Candidates were no longer interested in jobs that offered only monetary compensation. They demanded more—more job relatability, more training initiatives, more all-inclusive career growth, and thus more perceived security. They wanted to critically appraise the company's vision, market sensibilities, human-resource policies and strategies, growth opportunities, long term strategies towards learning and development, and past and present performance.

Three major developments took place that needed immediate attention and a single quick solution:

> The job market progressed from local to global as employers were now ready to hire the best talent available without any geographical constraint, while candidates were also more open to international relocation. At the same time, minimizing the hiring cost and the risk of a bad hire was vital.

> Interviews could no longer be a one-sided selection process. Hiring now had to be blended with sales to make it a mutual process to entice the best candidates.

> Candidates as well as companies wanted to ensure that the relationship would be based on long-term mutual trust and benefit.

The best solution to all of these issues: the telephone interview.

Telephone interviews – the key to saving time, effort, and money

A question naturally appeared in the minds of recruiters—as interviews consume a great amount of time, effort, and money, could the telephone interview be an effective solution? Could it be more than just an additional step in an already cumbersome process?

The two following flowcharts show the typical interview processes with and without telephonic rounds respectively. In this case, we assume that the telephone interview in question is not merely a pre-screening, but a well-conducted, detailed interview—the way it should ideally be and as it will be described in detail in the following chapters. The flowcharts clearly illustrate all the stages (based on high probability situations) in both types of processes, and also point out the steps at which resource wastage happens—the wastage points are noted by asterisks.

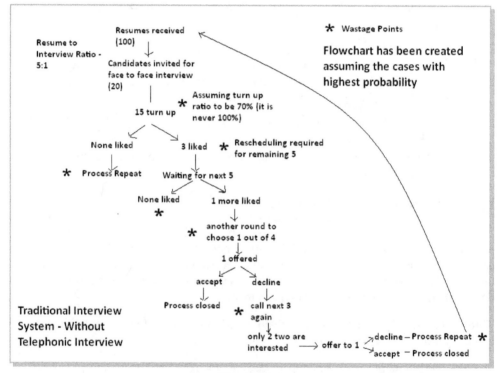

Flowchart 1.1

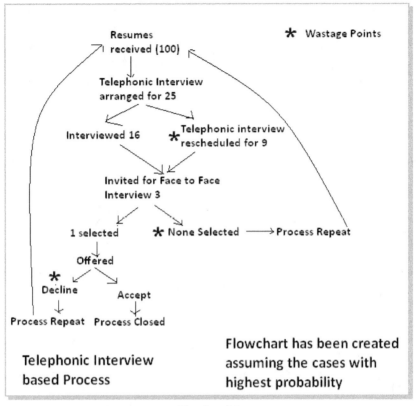

Flowchart 1.2

Two important observations can be made even from just a momentary glance at the two flowcharts:

➤ The telephone interview greatly reduces the number of steps in the recruitment process, ensuring faster recruitment for the open position.

➤ Chances of resource wastage are more probable in the traditional interview system

The following table presents the analysis of the wastage points shown in both the methods:

Traditional interview without telephonic round (Flowchart 1.1)	Telephone-interview-based process (Flowchart 1.2)
Arranging face-to-face interviews for 20 or more candidates is a big drain on resources.	Scheduling telephone interviews takes less time, as candidates can be available at any time during the day.
The probability of process failure is much higher in direct face-to-face interviews because of undisclosed expectations of both employer as well as employee.	Candidates who appear for a face-to-face interview have already been developed as prospects with great interest in the job opening. A telephone interview provides the candidates with the opportunity to refuse over the telephone if they are not interested.
All the related line managers and HR managers along with the support staff must be available for 15 candidates, taking an enormous amount of time away from other business interests.	Arranging three face-to-face interviews is less time consuming for everyone, more easily coordinated, less resource intensive, and more targeted.
Resources are wasted unnecessarily in rescheduling interviews for candidates who could not make the original date.	Rescheduling a telephone interview is relatively easy and can be dealt with comfortably.
The process cycle becomes so long and time consuming that the prospective candidate may lose interest or take an offer from a competitor.	The process cycle is shorter and more engaging, maintaining the candidate's interest. A shorter cycle also means quicker closure, beating the competition. Moreover, the sooner the employee is brought on board, the faster they can deliver the results.

One psychological reality that we must never ignore is that *when presented with 15 or more options face to face, it becomes very difficult to choose the best three* because the factors that should be pertinent only to face-to-face interviews integrate factors that are not dependent on physical presence. It complicates the power of strategic selection by creating a misunderstanding between what is being offered and what is required.

Finally, *Flowchart 1.1* shows the completion of the process; another strong possibility is that the recruiter will be left with only two alternatives. They may choose one of the remaining two candidates, compromising on quality by selecting a new hire who was never on the first priority list, or they can repeat the entire process cycle. Either way, it's going to be a massive depletion of resources in time, effort, man hours, and consequently money.

In the case of detailed telephone interviews, there is no body language or facial expression, and hence the focus is only on the voice and the answers of the candidate, and the conviction they carry. This is not the limitation it might seem at first. In fact, most of the important psychological and technical factors can and should be tested on the telephone. The face-to-face interview should judge only the factors that are vital to physical representation of the person, such as soft skills. This leads to a more logical process of selection. Hence, the chances of process failure and repetition are greatly diminished.

Developing prospects is essential

Gone are the days when money alone used to make an offer lucrative for the candidates. Post recession, candidates have become extremely sophisticated, as well as cautious before accepting any job opportunity. Two important realizations have resulted in sales and HR techniques joining forces and altering the traditional recruitment method.

Firstly, a candidate now scrutinizes the new organization, role, and management as closely as a recruiter examines the candidate. Candidates can be divided into two groups, as observed and explained:

> *"The first group is much quicker to accept things as they are and tries to maintain the status quo. They want a job where there is a sense of stability and potential growth opportunity, and they are more worried about being part of a larger team. Post-2008, this group has become even more focused on stability and long term security.*
>
> *The other group entered into the workforce just prior to 2008 or after; this group appears to have a much different dynamic. This group is not as concerned with "big companies", and is more focused on how the opportunity will benefit them."*

by Jason Carson, Director, Labor Relations/Human Resources and Safety, Brillion Iron Works, United States

In either case, the candidate holds many expectations of the recruiting company before thinking about whether to join their team, or not.

Secondly, companies have learned from their past experiences that *it's only the top performers who rise to the challenge during the worst times and keep the company afloat.* Hence, organizations are critically engaged in identifying such professionals and acquiring their services before their competitors can. So, top performers have top organizations and offers lining up for them.

Both these developments together have created the demand that has converted the recruitment process into a mutual selection process.

Prospect development through telephone interviews is extremely important because the candidate would not enter the interview venue without being absolutely sure about it. Because of this, the quality of telephone interview as well as the interviewer has come under scrutiny, and the interviewer and their pitch are the crucial factors in closing the deal, just like in a sales process.

Ergo, it is imperative for an organization to make sure that the telephone-interview process is strong, logical, and far reaching, and that the interviewer is proficiently skilled to carry out this process. The following chapters will equip you to do all that is required to master this art; but before that, one must be able to spot the errors that are currently being made in the selection process.

Summary

The recession has made a large impact on the way recruitment processes are initially carried out, leading to a complete process transition. Candidates and organizations have become more watchful and are aiming to save time and money while also creating a long-term and mutually beneficial relationship.

Telephone interviews offer a solution to the companies as well as candidates in delivering the results they demand by shortening the recruitment process and making it more cost efficient—converting the recruitment process into a qualitative process of mutual selection.

The aftermath of the recession has taught employers and employees alike the consequences of money-based relationships that were created in haste. The telephone interview provides all the participants a chance to effectively compare their respective requirements and expectations, simultaneously offering a platform for a more stable relationship.

The next chapter will enable you to revise the way in which telephone interviews are being conducted within your organization currently, and will help you to identify the mistakes that are weakening the process.

>2

Are You Doing It Correctly?

During my long experience, I have witnessed global organizations such as GE, ARM, and American Express adapting quickly to the demands of revolutionizing business trends. That includes redesigning their recruitment process, which is now based on an efficient telephone-interview round. However, a large number of organizations are still treating the telephone interview only as a preliminary screening process. When it is used only to check the basic soft skills of a candidate, a telephone interview fails to provide a holistic view at either end. As a result, neither the candidate nor the recruiter is sure about their relationship until they meet. An opportunity is wasted.

Before I started to write this book, I conducted a survey of 800 employees who had faced at least three telephone interviews in the last year. Every candidate had faced at least one telephone interview in which:

> ➤ The interview lasted for about five to seven minutes

> ➤ The candidate felt that only their communication skills were tested, and even then only superficially

> ➤ There was no discussion about role clarity

> ➤ Candidates were never given a chance to ask any questions, unless the candidate specifically requested the opportunity

> ➤ Finally, availability for a face-to-face interview was checked

The survey results clearly demonstrate that there is often a frustrating lack of essential interest and planning when developing this interview step, a step that can be hugely rewarding in such demanding times.

Case study

Jason approached his phone to call Helen, an Institutional Sales Manager from their closest competitor, well known for her performance, for a telephone interview. It was around 4 pm, and it had been a busy Monday for Helen. She was in the middle of designing a PowerPoint presentation when her cell phone buzzed. Reluctantly, she answered the call. Jason began by telling her who he was and that he wanted to ask a few questions, but Helen had to interrupt him and politely decline his request. He was asked to call again after the office hours were over, to which he reluctantly agreed.

Around 7 pm, Jason called Helen again. Suddenly, he realized that he had forgotten her resume at the office, so he was not left with much to ask. This time Helen was prepared for his questions, but to her dismay, there weren't many.

Jason broke the ice with the most commonly asked question, "Please, tell me about yourself?" As she started speaking, he ran to another room to pick up a pen and piece of paper. He managed to scribble a few things. With his attention divided between listening, jotting notes, and arranging his papers, he could not decide what to ask next.

Finally, he rescued himself by asking, "Are you aware of the position you applied for?". Well, after replying "Yes", Helen was expecting more from Jason when he concluded the interview by simply asking her availability for a face-to-face interview.

Helen put the phone down bemused, requesting a day's time to think and confirm.

Jason was left frustrated; after all, he had been following her since the morning and was still unsure as to what her decision would be.

What went wrong?

Try to recall if you ever put down the phone with the same frustration that Jason suffered. You were confused and could not make out what the candidate expected. You kept wondering what was wrong with the interview.

If you reflect on your past experiences, you will find that more than 60 percent of such interviews resulted in disinterested candidates who never confirmed for a face-to-face interview. In some cases, where the candidate was a known performer, someone senior from your company had to intervene and convince the candidate for a face-to-face meeting.

So, the same question crops up again. What went wrong? Let's try and find out the answer to this haunting dilemma by considering the following questions.

Did you plan ahead?

"By failing to prepare, you are preparing to fail"

-Benjamin Franklin, Founding Father of the United States of America

The significance of planning couldn't be more plainly put than it was by Benjamin Franklin. The goal may be as big as winning a battle or as small as interviewing a job candidate, but the course to success always starts with effective planning.

In fact, for an organization, interviewing a prospective candidate is nothing less than winning a battle—a battle against its competitors to win the best resources available. The outcome of a simple mistake in the hiring process can be catastrophic, with the person whom we wanted to work for us now working against us. Further results of my previously mentioned survey indicate that more than 72 percent of interviewees felt that the interviewer had not properly prepared. This had an impact on the respondent's decision to move ahead with the process in 58 percent of cases.

In the case mentioned previously, the lack of planning is apparent at each step, starting from Jason making an impromptu call. Ideally, Jason should have fixed up an appointment through e-mail or SMS so that Helen was prepared for his call. Instead, he caught her in the middle of her work, unaware, which certainly must have left her unhappy. This was not the only error that he made. Forgetting to carry her resume, improper and inadequate questioning, and not being ready with a pen and piece of paper were all factors in the greatest devil of interviewing—no planning.

But what, usually, do we plan for? We plan for the things that we consider important to ourselves—the tasks in which we want to deliver successful results—the processes we take seriously.

Lack of planning comes from misjudgment and failure to appreciate the value of the telephone interview for its own sake. We expect candidates to approach each step of the interview process with equal earnestness. But sometimes, we end up not giving enough weight to our processes. That creates a situation of disorder and disconnection.

The notion Helen must have drawn was that the company does not have well-defined processes. Additionally, though this process could have created a genuine interest from her for the company as well as the role, it failed to do so because her mind was still full of questions regarding the role, company, culture, and most importantly, her own future in light of these factors.

Finally, her mind was still asking "What was this interview for?".

Check your telephone etiquette

Any form of communication can be considered complete only when the objectives of that communication are met. The more complicated a communication skill, the greater articulation it requires. Telephone conversations are a complex form of communication in which achieving the goals set is easier said than done.

The principal problem with this type of communication is that the parties engaged cannot see each other. There are no handshakes, facial expressions, or hand gestures; no body language, eye contact, nor any other supporting feature that can cover up any mistakes that our words or tone make. In a face-to-face conversation, even if we end up making a bad start, we can still start working for a better end. Our body, holistically, works in unison with our words to provide all-inclusive support to our thought processes and helps put our message across to the listener in the most stimulating manner.

Telephone conversation, however, is an entirely different ball game. It's not only about what we say but also how we say it. Since the person at the other end can't see us, they start to paint a picture of us in their mind right from the first word we speak. Candidates often begin telephone interviews with a great deal of apprehension. If the first impression the interviewer can conjure with voice alone is a good one, it reassures an applicant about their decision to interview and generates a curiosity to meet.

Make a note

 A telephone interview is yet another business deal, the success of which depends on the mutual respect and admiration developed through professional and well articulated conversation between two people representing different organizations and their respective cultures, towards a common objective of meeting to explore the opportunity to work together for mutual benefit.

Remember that an interviewer represents not only themselves but an organization and its values, principles, and culture; a good interviewer will leave a long-lasting and positive impression on the job applicant. The survey showed that for 78 percent of candidates, the telephone mannerisms and communication skills of the interviewer influenced their decision to attend the face-to-face interview.

But how do we make certain that each time we conduct a telephone interview with a prospective employee, especially the one that is on our management's top priority list, the result is a meaningful relationship based on mutual trust and benefit?

Simple! By making the best display of telephone etiquette and mannerisms.

"Good manners will open doors that the best education cannot."

-Clarence Thomas, Associate Justice of the Supreme Court of the United States of America

We can safely say that the mental picture that an applicant has drawn of us, and consequently the organization that we represent, is a good one if we can epitomize the qualities explored in the following sections.

Be sensitive

Start with scheduling the call, keeping the mutual convenience of the call in mind. We must never ignore the fact that the person we are calling is firstly an employee of their present company and only later a job applicant. While in their current job, they still have to carry out their responsibilities as dutifully as possible, and an interview will always come second to that. Make sure that you call only at a mutually-agreed and prescheduled date and time, which can be arranged through e-mails or SMS. Even if you are calling at an approved time, it's no harm to reconfirm the candidate's availability to be sure of their undivided attention. Additionally, in the context of global hiring, different time zones must be kept in mind while coordinating the telephone interviews.

Be cordial

Have you ever felt that someone's friendly "Good evening" made you feel alive at the end of a tough working day? Suddenly, it changes our perception about the day. We no longer see it as an end to a stressful day but a great start to a relieving evening. Similarly, start your call with a smile, as smiling is reflected in your tone and puts the other person at ease. Giving comfort and being pleasant subtly forces the candidate to be more candid, eventually making the process more fruitful.

Be attentive

If you don't seem to pay attention to the candidate, why should they pay attention to you? A candidate can be as interested in joining us as we would be interested in hiring. Being alert comes with its own set of benefits. It communicates to the candidates that we are really interested in exploring the chances of this relationship. It exhibits our level of preparedness and invites the candidate to take us seriously. Finally, it empowers us to judge the interview process and the candidate accurately and discover anything incongruous.

Be natural

If your words aren't getting your meaning across, it is indicative of some essential divide between what we said and the way it was being understood (or misunderstood). The problem could be one of accent, or it could be down to the use of idiomatic language or a slang. If you are not being understood, it is better to rephrase than to simply repeat. We are in dynamic times where hiring must have a global reach. Simple and straightforward English with a neutral accent is best as it can be easily comprehended by professionals across the world. Using strong vocabulary is one of the biggest hindrances to effective communication. After all, we want the incoming employee to be an effective communicator and not a novel writer. So, we must hold off our urge to use difficult vocabulary, unless interviewing for a role that demands strong vocabulary. Keep it simple!

Be distinct

If you think that the other person is very loud, first check yourself. Is your loudness compelling them to match your tone? A shrieking voice can be intimidating, while a timid one suggests the speaker is low on either confidence or content. Either way, it's not good for the process. Ideally, a telephone interview establishes a platform based on mutual interaction. Being either too loud or too soft will make the candidate either fear or pity you. Pay attention from the start of the conversation, and modulate your volume so that the person you are talking to can easily identify the words and correctly interpret the meaning.

Be expressive

A good discussion fosters interest. The greater the interest, the greater the understanding of each other. The better the understanding, the greater the willingness to explore the means to strengthen the relationship. The higher the willingness, the greater the chances of success. Monotony is the biggest killer of an interesting conversation. If you chose to be monotonous, chances are that your conversation partner will want to put the phone down as soon as possible. That would be absolutely detrimental to a relationship that could be so fertile in future. Since the telephone isolates your body language from conversation, tone modulation is the only way you can keep your listener interested. All the enthusiastic gestures in the world won't help your cause if you can't communicate them through your tone of voice.

Having said all that, do not forget about one extremely important aspect of any conversation, especially on the telephone—listening. Actively listening. The gravity of this skill is so high that I felt a great need to discuss it separately, because the success of a telephone interview fundamentally depends on how much we listen, not how much we speak.

How well did you listen?

Irrespective of the number of training sessions, books, websites, blogs, or any other sources advocating the prominence of listening skills, we incessantly choose to ignore them. The main culprit is our reduced concentration span. We are always in a hurry to speak our minds, as our thoughts multiply and race more quickly than we can handle. 81 percent of respondents in my survey strongly believed in the contribution of the interviewer's listening skills towards successful results. Conversely, 67 percent felt that during one of the telephone interviews they faced, the attention of the recruiter was divided; that is, there was no **active listening**.

Several irritating distractions during the interview process were cited by the interviewees: the interviewer attending to their cell phone, talking to or being interrupted by another colleague, cell phone network disturbances, and munching or chewing were the most common culprits. Lack of planning has the same result, as it muddles up the interviewer and pulls their concentration away from the candidate's responses.

In Jason's case, the first panic signs appeared when he realized he had forgotten the resume, and were made worse by his not having a pen and a piece of paper handy. Jason went on looking for the things he needed while Helen had already started speaking. It's quite obvious that Jason was distracted from the important task of listening to Helen while part of his attention was focused on the things he'd forgotten.

Even after he realized he'd forgotten the resume, the interview needn't have been a lost cause had Jason reacted differently. Jason could have compensated for the missing resume by effectively listening to Helen and creating opportunities to ask more open-ended questions. Additionally, several other opportunities for listening could be created, such as asking about her expectations from the new organization and job, as he didn't need her resume for that.

Asking more questions and listening actively to her would have helped him to:

> ➤ Survey and probe her thoughts on her profession
> ➤ Identify her professional and personal goals
> ➤ Secure his relationship with her
> ➤ Curtail any misunderstandings or confusion
> ➤ Successfully call her for the next interview step based on the trust established

Unfortunately, Jason did none of this, and needlessly lost a valuable opportunity.

All that we have addressed so far is the problem, so let's try and find out if there could be a solution as well. Effective listening, like any other other communication skill, can't be attained overnight. One must start by recognizing its importance, then it must be practiced, followed by continual assessment, and then still more practice.

A few tips that may come in handy while practicing are explored in the following sections.

Prepare adequately

A well-planned task is a task already half-done. Active listening needs a clutter-free mind. Effective planning is essential. Once we have our tools ready—and that includes mental preparation as well as the basics like pen and paper—there won't be any need to worry about them. No worries means great concentration, which facilitates active listening.

Avoid distractions

Being well prepared improves your concentration. Planning ahead to avoid distractions—or training yourself to ignore them—will push your concentration up another notch. Distractions or interruptions disrupt the continuity of conversation. A disarrayed mind will greatly reduce the quality of what could be a rewarding discussion. Additionally, it shows a lackadaisical attitude and lack of respect.

Demonstrate genuine interest

Nothing can win over a candidate more than genuine interest. Be truly engaged in the conversation, which can only be achieved through active participation. Don't simply ask questions and wait for the answer. Keep showing your presence and engagement with an occasional "alright", "great", and "right".

Ask open-ended questions

Open-ended questions are highly instrumental in extracting the best possible information. A question like "Are you interested in joining our company?" could only fetch a simple yes or no. However, asking "What do you expect from our company in order to create your sustained interest in this job?" would force the candidate to speak more about their feelings and expectations, providing a more detailed picture.

Never jump to conclusions

Because of our extensive experience with interviews, we develop a tendency to jump to conclusions, even before a candidate completes their answer. Wait! Don't presume that you know what a candidate is going to say before they've said it, and don't offer your own opinion until you're sure you've absolutely understood the perspective the candidate has offered you. Never interrupt the candidates while they are answering a question with your own understanding of the situation. If they take a moment to compose their thoughts, resist the temptation to offer them the answer you expect to hear. Doing so will always hide the true nature and meaning of the candidates' responses.

Assess regularly

Deterioration of listening skills is a gradual process. Regular assessment of what we're doing and how we're doing it enables us to weed out the common mistakes that we make during conversations with respect to listening. Now, how many of us actually do that— regular assessment? I am sure just a handful, and I am in no doubt that numbers would be lower for those who have a "formal process of listening skills assessment". Of course, an assessment helps, but it truly achieves its objectives only when it's regular and formal. What I mean by "formal" is a standard checklist which one must tick regularly—this can be benchmarked against the required standards.

Action Point

Work through the following checklist and develop a formal format for assessing your listening skills. You can customize the template to meet your specific requirements.

Telephonic Interview Listening Skills - Assessment Checklist

While conducting telephonic Interview, I	Correct	Incorrect
Always plan adequately, including the time of call	☐	☐
Be at a quiet place during interview	☐	☐
Keep candidate's resume, accompanied by a candidate assessment form	☐	☐
Never chew or drink, except an occasional glass of water	☐	☐
keep my cell phone away from the landline to avoid signal disturbances	☐	☐
Never Check my cell phone for messages or emails	☐	☐
Never Check my email inbox	☐	☐
Never Allow colleagues to talk to me	☐	☐
Keep my list of questions ready	☐	☐
Ask more of open-ended questions	☐	☐
always keep my mind focussed	☐	☐
Never Interrupt the candidate in the middle of an answer with my thoughts	☐	☐
Also focus on non verbal communication like tone modulation	☐	☐
Make appropriate notes	☐	☐
Listen without jumping to conclusions	☐	☐
Encourage the candidate to speak more	☐	☐

An active telephonic interview listerner should be able to check all of them 'Correct'

Assessment Date: _____
Time of Interview: _____

Interviewer's Name: _____
Candidate's name: _____
Position Interviewed For: _____

Did you record it?

You planned it properly, asked relevant questions, and overall had a good interview session, but did you record it? In a telephone interview especially, there is a high chance that certain important verbal or non-verbal elements are left unanalyzed. This could be down to several factors. Did any of the following keep you from making an accurate record:

➤ Uncontrollable distractions, such as a call from your manager

➤ A temporary and slight drift in your attention during the interview

➤ Too long a discussion

➤ Disturbance in the telephone connection

➤ Noisy background at the candidate's end

➤ Network issues at the candidate's end

If any of this happened, and the interviewer was not recording the call in some form or another, it is highly probable that the assessment of the interview session or the candidate may be flawed, resulting in great wastage of effort at both ends.

One of the worst ways of recording the notes of a telephone interview session is by scribbling on the resume itself. Scribbles are mostly illegible, lack complete information, and do not act as a checklist. If the interview is conducted by two to three people in an organization, one person's scribble will often be useless for others. Combining the perspectives of two to three people would be very difficult as well, enhancing the chances of errors. A properly established recording mechanism is a must.

The notes should be made clearly on a separate sheet of paper, stapled to the resume after the interview. There are two defined approaches, the combination of which will not only provide a detailed interview record, but will also act as a tool for benchmarking against required capabilities.

Record the conversation

Technology has empowered us so much that the entire telephone conversation can be recorded by the simple push of a button on our telephone.

Recording is useful because it safeguards against the loss of information caused by any of the distractions discussed previously. Furthermore, it provides us with an opportunity to listen to the entire conversation again to check if something passed us by undetected. If you decide to record an interview, always make sure that the candidate is informed in advance.

Candidate assessment checklist

Proper planning will mean you are already clear about the capabilities you are looking for in a prospective employee. Make an assessment checklist and create an interlinked questionnaire. Tick each assessment criterion as the interview progresses. Not only will this add clarity to your process, it also facilitates an easy comparison between the feedback of different interviewing authorities. In one step, you've made clearer notes, cut down on writing during the interview, and devised a mechanism for making collective judgments.

If you think something is missing, you still have the recording with you, don't you?

Did you sell the job?

The economic quagmire has reached its zenith and the apprehension levels of employees have risen with it. Financial worries remain an issue of grave importance.

Selling the job is all about making sure that the candidate knows all the challenges and incentives of joining an organization before taking the next step. Joining a new job and organization is in itself a big challenge, which will affect their future directly. Facilitating them in getting all the relevant information about the job, the organization, and its relevant policies plays a significant role in earning the trust of the candidate. It establishes transparency in the transactions and clarity in the objectives imbued in the vision of an organization.

Selling the job is important not only from the candidate's perspective, but is also worth mentioning in the context of the organization. In such a cut-throat competitive scenario, when every organization is focused on hiring the best talent, recruiters are facing a severe struggle to get hold of the right resource—an employee for whom money is not the only important factor but who sees their career and the company's progression as interlinked. Transparency and clarity only aids in achieving this.

However, recruiters must avoid "misselling". Almost 56 percent of survey participants reported that they were misled at some point in their careers by recruiters who painted rosy pictures about the future growth avenues for the organization as well as for their job. Remember that false commitments can damage your brand image in the market. Misselling can lead to a stage where nobody of high enough caliber wants to be associated with your company, so avoid it at all costs.

Pressure to hire a performer sometimes leads the recruiter in the wrong direction. This pressure can be relieved by offering a clear picture limited to their job requirements. After all, the candidate is also supposed to carry out their own research. Moreover, the entire process can be facilitated, in a restrictive fashion, by inviting candidates to ask questions. Answer the questions truthfully with the facts and let them form their own judgment. That way, they will always feel like a decision-maker, while in actual fact you will be leading the negotiation.

The reform

In the light of the entire discussion, let's see what changes Jason needs to make in order to win over Helen's candidature.

Jason approached his phone as he was supposed to call Helen at 6 pm for an interview. She was an Institutional Sales Manager from their closest competitor, well known for her performance.

Jason found her waiting for his call. Jason greeted her with a smile in his voice, introduced himself, and asked for her permission to record the conversation.

He was ready with her resume, pen, and a notepad with all other necessary documents. He started with carefully selected questions, inquiring in depth about her career growth, education history, past performance, market knowledge, and several other relevant indicators.

As she was answering his questions, he listened intently and made important notes on the designated form. After being satisfied with her answers, he told her about the role, responsibilities, and future career progression possibilities, before finally inviting her to ask questions, if she had any.

In the end, he requested her to check her calendar and inform him about her availability so that he could arrange an interview with other members of the recruitment team. He also told her about the next steps and ended the call with a warm "goodbye", also reminding her that he would expect her reply soon.

Jason was relieved because he was confident about Helen's candidature and hopeful about her interest.

Did I miss something? Oh, Helen's reaction! You tell me. If you were Helen, would you like to explore this opportunity?

Summary

We have seen that planning is an essential element and a guiding factor of the interview process. As per the survey, more than 72 percent of participants reported lack of planning in the telephone interview they faced, which had an adverse impact upon the decision to move ahead with the opportunity.

Telephone etiquette is vital in establishing a positive connection between the interviewer and interviewee. A clear, cordial, and undistracted telephone conversation must be targeted in order to achieve a mutually beneficial communication.

For a telephone interview to be successful, it is important for the recruiter to speak less and listen more. Hence, a careful selection of open-ended questions supported by the interviewer's skillful **active listening** aids in the development of mutual trust and respect. It also assures both parties that they are moving in the right direction.

A systematic and results-oriented recording, documentation, and assessment mechanism should be developed and formally implemented throughout the organization leadership. It will aid the ongoing assessment and develop the telephone interview as a practice recognized for its productivity.

Sell your company, the job, and try to create the opportunity for a successful association by providing the relevant information to the candidate. Invite the candidate to ask questions pertaining to the job and the company, but do not over-sell or missell, as it tarnishes the brand image of the company.

In the next chapter, you will be able to learn exactly how to plan, conduct, and assess a telephone interview, along with learning the right approach to successfully sell the job.

> 3

Plan, Conduct, and Assess

This is where we put our theories and conceptual understanding to the test. In this chapter, we will learn how to plan at macro and micro levels, to take a stepwise approach to successfully conducting a telephone interview, examine the right ways to appraise a candidate, and finally how to evaluate the candidate's skills in light of the job requirements.

How to plan a telephone interview

We have already discussed at great length how acting without planning makes the path to success difficult. Creating a rational plan eliminates system failures. Fleming's concept of Total Quality Management (TQM) teaches us that planning on macro as well as micro levels is crucial to make a business robust in the face of any individual shortcomings.

Macro-planning provides us with perspective and goals. It establishes the underlined purpose behind what we intend to do. Micro-planning highlights the resources and plan of action needed for its execution.

Macro-planning

Since a telephone interview is a very thorny process, it is a necessity for macro-planning to define its goals and purpose. We have already seen how a mishandled telephone interview can lead to irrecoverable losses. While macro-planning, a recruiter must recognize the process in light of three progressive stages.

Action Point

Look at the interviewer's planning form given as follows. Consider how you would frame these answers for your own hiring goals, bearing in mind the key points in this chapter.

Telephonic Interviewer's Planning Form

Position concerned: _____   Type of opening: (New or Replacement) _____

Department: _____   Last person holding this position, if any _____

Department Head or the Team Leader: _____

Purpose of Hiring	Specific Requirements of this Position

What is expected of the candidate at this position?

The skills to focus upon

Questions to be asked

Purpose behind the hiring

A hiring requirement comes from the line managers or team leaders. Recruiters must be able to assess the purpose of hiring clearly. In the course of doing so, they must always be able to ask the right questions: why has this position come up? Is it a newly-created position or a replacement hire? Why did the previous person leave? Was there a problem with the person who left, or with the requirements of this position? The recruiter must discuss these issues and try to get specific guidance from the line manager on what the team requires.

Make a note

It is much easier for recruiters to understand the requirements of the position when the purpose of hiring is established. When hiring to replace someone who has left a post, recruiters should be able to diagnose whether there was a problem with the person or with the position. They must know what characteristics they are now looking for that the last person lacked or that the job now demands. This may simply require a casual tête-à-tête with the manager.

Expectations from the candidate

Establishing the purpose of a hire and analyzing the needs of the post will pin down your expectations of the ideal candidate. Now the recruiter can tell, in definite terms, what they should be looking for. Be methodical and ask structured questions that will allow you to assess applicants based on the qualities you know you need.

The Tolstoy Trap

William D. Eggers and John O'Leary call it "The Tolstoy Trap". In their book *If We Can Put a Man on the Moon*, they cite one of Tolstoy's most famous maxims:

> *"The simplest thing cannot be made clear to the most intelligent man if he is firmly persuaded that he knows already, without a shadow of doubt, what is laid before him."*

> *–Leo Tolstoy*

I believe that in most cases, it is this trap that leads to either no plans or failed plans. Recruiters tend to assume that they already know all there is to know. If it's a sales position, then they will focus only upon the sales-related issues. They never try to find out if there is something else that caused this vacancy. These recruiters are never even aware that there are other factors that they also need to judge—such as regional knowledge. If they try to find out and get hold of the real reason for the hire, they will be able to address all the issues—even those that were at first — and solve the puzzle in a rational manner.

Micro-planning

Micro-planning aids in the identification and development of accurate tools. Once we know what we are looking for (thanks to macro-planning), it is easier to find it it. However, identifying what one needs but then being unable to obtain it is immensely frustrating, such as finding a limited-stock piece of jewelry you love at 50 percent sale, only to realize that you aren't carrying enough money to buy it. This is where micro-planning comes in.

A good interview is a well-defined and organized process. You have every opportunity to plan ahead and avoid any such catastrophe. Small details matter. Let's prepare a checklist.

Scheduling the interview

It all starts with thoughtful scheduling of the interview. There are several things that a recruiter must consider when scheduling an interview. Ensure that the time of the call is pre-arranged with the candidate. Use e-mail to schedule the call so they can consider their reply. Block your calendar and set a reminder so that there is no mix up at your end. If it's a panel interview, it must be arranged with great care so as to make certain that all the participants are free and available and able to give their undivided attention. Select the quietest corner in your office or book a meeting room in advance. Check the telephone lines and the recording system and be certain that they are working. Don't forget to send a reminder to the entire panel so that everyone is ready at the time of the interview with a pen and notepad.

Keeping all the documents ready

A copy of the resume and all the relevant assessment forms, along with copy of the job description that was sent to the candidate, must be available to all the interviewers. You should also make sure that the candidate has a copy of the job description and encourage them to have it to hand during the interview.

Preparing your list of questions

Remember that an interview is all about getting the answers to the relevant questions. The keyword here is **relevant**. We already know the purpose of this hiring, understand the requirement completely, and have an idea of what exactly we are looking for. Carefully selecting the list of appropriate questions completes our planning process. Now all we have to do is be prepared to listen.

Make a note

A simple way to avoid leaving anything unplanned for is to prepare a checklist. I am providing a sample checklist. You can use it as a template to prepare your own.

Telephonic Interview Planning Checklist

Candidate's Name: _____   Date and Time for Interview: _____

Position Considered For: _____   Interviewers: _____

Department: _____

Checklist	Yes	No
Do I understand the purpose of the hiring?		
Do I know the requirements of the job?		
Have I listed the expectations from the candidate at this position?		
Has the candidate confirmed the availability at given date and time?		
Does the candidate has the detailed job description to be prepared?		
Are all the interviewers informed and reminded about the interview date and time?		
Does everyone has a copy of the resume?		
Does every interviewer has a copy of relevant assessment forms?		
Is the telephone and recording apparatus ready?		
Is the conference room booking done and confirmed?		
Does the entire hiring team has a copy of job description that was sent to the candidate?		
Am I ready with my list of questions?		
Have I double checked that my list of questions contains mostly open-ended questions and are highly relevant to the candidate as well as the position concerned?		
Most importantly, does every interviewer knows that it is a telephonic interview, understands it gravity and is prepared adequately as per the norms of telephonic interview?		

If the answer to any of the aforementioned questions is 'No', then you are not yet ready to conduct the telephonic interview and need time to prepare.

How to conduct a successful telephonic interview

Planning is useless if it's not put into action. While preparing for an interview, a recruiter should never disregard the fact that the exclusive purpose of an interview is to get the maximum information out of the applicant and to ensure that most of it is true. Of course, a few things are cross-checked through references, but most of it can be derived by a cognitive analysis of the candidate's answers.

In a face-to-face interview, it is easier to catch lies and dig out information if the body language or the non-verbal communication does not support a candidate's words. In telephone interviews, without body language or facial expressions, it becomes all the more difficult. However, it can still be achieved to a great extent if a recruiter builds a rapport with the interviewee.

Building a rapport with a candidate whom you have never seen or heard before on your first telephone conversation? It may sound difficult, but in fact it is simply a skill that can be learned. How many recruiters actually begin their interviews by saying, "Your resume looks great, and I am sure that we will have a great interview"?

Make the interviewee comfortable with a warm greeting and a smile. The candidate may not be able to see it, but they can certainly feel it in your tone. Keep your tone moderate and make sure that both of you are on the same wavelength. If you work smartly at this, you won't find it too hard to sell your job in the end. Having discussed this in great detail in *Chapter 2, Are You Doing It Correctly?*, now let's turn our attention to the other essentials of conducting an interview.

Open-ended questions

Expert and seasoned interviewers like Claudio Fernandez-Araoz have widely observed that in most interview cases, it is the interviewer who speaks more. Ideally, it should be the interviewee who does the lion's share of the talking. Listening skills have already been emphasized, but no matter how strong the emphasis is, it can never be enough. It must be an active process. One method for effective listening is to ask targeted but open-ended questions. A simple example could be asking "What is your opinion about this role?" instead of "Are you interested in this role?". The candidate will be forced to speak their mind about the role, rather than simply answering a yes or no.

An interview is well conducted if it highlights all the aspects that we were seeking. Questions are asked to reveal patterns related to a professional and personal thought process. The questions that a recruiter must ask (and should preferably ask in the order given) can be broadly classified into the following five categories.

Work-related questions

This section can be segregated into two parts: factual information about the candidate's current role and organization, and the candidate's understanding and management of their work. It may include questions related to their current and previous employment; current roles and responsibilities; challenges faced in the current role and the candidate's way of managing them; accomplishments and failures; their relationship with their manager; and, most importantly, the reason they are looking for a change. The answers to these questions will tell us about the candidate's understanding of their job, their organization, and the way they view and gel with their team. This also validates the reason behind the job change and tells us the key points upon which we may sell the job if the candidate is selected.

Candidate-centric questions

These questions aim to uncover the candidate's viewpoint about their professional and personal attitude. Starting with how a candidate manages a typical day or week, questions can move on to cover their basic lifestyle and work/life balance, the way they handle stress and work pressures, and their self-motivation. Further questions may focus on their biggest strengths and weaknesses, their driving passions, their decision-making capability, and many other intertwined personal and professional traits.

Questions about the new job and organization

These questions are specially designed to discover the level of research the candidate has performed and the degree of awareness that they possess of your expectations. The overall understanding about the role and responsibilities in the new job is judged. This can also measure the level of excitement a candidate possesses about taking up the role. Asking them specifically about the challenges they are expecting will enable the recruiters to assess if the job and candidate complement each other.

The candidate's vision

A professional must have a meticulous and pragmatic route map to their goals, because in the end, a comprehensive professional performance and a balanced personal life complete the definition of success. Asking questions such as, "Where do you see yourself ten years down the line?", and "How do you plan to achieve this goal?", or "How do you think this job may help you in achieving your goals?" will push the candidate to think and reveal clearly the way they imagine their future might shape up.

Behavioral questions

Behavioral questions are extremely important in determining the way a candidate behaves in a given situation. Such questions are essentially useful in evaluating the environment in which the candidate has been cultured and comparing that to the work culture of your organization. These questions must be tailored to the recruiter's specific needs, and demand that the candidate comes up with an impromptu answer that reflects strongly their own set of thoughts and behaviors.

Make a note

These questions do tell you a lot of what you need to know about any candidate and don't require the candidate to be physically present. You can evaluate all of this in a good telephone interview.

How to be a lie detector

Claiming to be a good performer during an interview and being able to substantiate this claim are two different things. Recruiters must frame their questions in a manner that demands the candidates provide evidence for whatever they claim. Recruiters of organizations that have already experienced the results of bad hires have become extremely cautious and are continuously developing interviewing techniques that enable them to uncover the truth about a candidate.

How can you tell if a candidate is trying to mislead you? There may not be a 100 percent-effective solution. After all, it's a contest between two minds. However, the person who is more prepared and can better manipulate the conversation will generally tip the scales in their favor. Well, we can't predict or control the interviewee's manipulation skills, but we can certainly firm up our preparations. Besides the basic issues of performance and capabilities, organizations now focus a lot on cultural and behavioral issues in hiring. Assessing a person's fit with the present company culture when working with teams, managers, departments, and, most importantly, the customers has become a top priority. Hence, a process must be developed to repeatedly ensure that the candidate did not tell them lies.

Here's a method you might try: offer very similar scenarios to the candidate at different intervals. Observe any contradictions in their answers. This may indicate that they are not being entirely candid. For example, you can assess the employee-manager relationship by asking "How is your relationship with your manager?". In all probability, the candidate is already prepared with an answer. A little later, ask a less-conventional question: "Describe an incident when you were not comfortable with your manager's decision and the way you managed that", for example, or "Have you ever been in a situation where your manager took credit for work you had done?". This forces the candidate to come up with an impromptu answer, and they might spill out something really important—something that they were not prepared for. In such cases, there are only three possibilities:

> ➤ The candidate is extremely well prepared and has another invention to hand
> ➤ The candidate is gifted with an excellent presence of mind to be able to come up with great impromptu answers, which may not be true
> ➤ The reality will be revealed

The last outcome is the most usual. Even if it's not, either the truth comes out during the reference check or at least you know that you did your best.

How to do a candidate assessment

A candidate assessment—the end target—can be accomplished if the interview is systematically recorded. The value of recording the interview can never be ignored. Through a series of questions, a recruiter tries to create a holistic image of the person interviewed—both as a person and a professional. The recruiter tries to figure out a person's cultural background; their social and ethical attributes. Furthermore, they inspect things such as teamwork, situation-handling, and decision-making capability. This holistic overview can be divided into smaller components on which the recruiter can form judgments.

Academic excellence

This consists of the evaluation of the academic achievements of the interviewee by cross-questioning them about their qualifications, their level of interest in particular relevant subjects, and the theoretical foundation of those subjects.

Profile relevance

This involves determining whether the profile of the candidate and the current role they work in matches the new role offered, or if the experience the candidate possesses warrants giving them new or greater responsibilities.

Market and industry knowledge

This involves judging the level of knowledge the candidate holds about the market and the industry as a whole. How well have they observed the dynamics of this industry? Do they understand the regional requirements or not? Do they have a clear picture of the customers' expectations from this industry, company, and product?

Business knowledge and understanding of the job profile

How well does the candidate understand the business nuances in this particular industry, market, or product line? This includes awareness of the general market and business practices, the challenges and rewards of this industry, and any other information that the candidate must possess in order to perform in this particular line of business. Moreover, the candidate must also be able to rightly assess the dedicated requirements of the new role to match the company's vision and objectives.

Personality traits

This deals with the prospective employee's strengths and weaknesses and the way they are handled by the candidate. How serious is the candidate towards their personal goals and is there pragmatism behind their plans to achieve them? This also reflects on how planned and organized a candidate is and the value of this new job offer in their personal and professional action plan.

Behavior and culture

This is the assessment of a candidate's role in a company as a contributor, team player, or team leader; their attitude towards their manager, management, and other team members; their conflict avoidance and resolution techniques; and any other significant behavior that affects their work performance, as well as their position within the team, directly or indirectly.

Methodical recording is absolutely necessary for properly making these assessments. A systematic process allows you to segregate out data you need and to ask questions accordingly. A simple candidate assessment sheet is a simple and effective way to keep track. Following is a customizable template for your candidate assessment sheet. Use it to record the candidate's traits in specific terms instead of simply tagging it as good or bad:

Telephonic Interview - Candidate Assessment Sheet

Candidate's Name: ———————————   Date and Time for Interview: ———————————

Position Considered For: ———————————   Department: ———————————

Assessment Reviews

Education	Profile

Market and Industry Knowledge	Business Knowhow and Understanding of the Job Profile

Personality Traits	Behavior and Culture

Special Comments, If Any

Interviewer's Name : ———————————

How to sell the job

By the end of the entire process, at least the following two things should become crystal clear:

➤ Is this job keen to have this candidate?

➤ Does this candidate really want this job?

We can keep interviewing the prospective candidates till we get a "Yes" for the first question. The moment the answer to the first question changes to "Yes", our next task is to convert the lead and call for a face-to-face interview in order to be able to close the deal. The possible combinations of answers to the previous questions are as follows:

➤ Yes—Yes

➤ Yes—No

If it's the former, then consider the candidate convinced to attend a face-to-face interview. Barring unforeseen factors, you already have a solid candidate for your post from the telephone interview stage alone. But what about the second scenario? In this case, you know from the telephone interview that you really want to meet the candidate face-to-face; however, the candidate does not seem too enthusiastic. What do you do?

Once the candidate has finished answering all the questions, they also expect a chance to ask a few questions, the answers to which will help them decide positively or negatively about the job and the company. The first step towards the successful promotion of a job by the recruiter is to answer all such questions candidly. This wins a candidate's trust, presenting both the recruiter and the organization as transparent and honest. Listening to the questions asked by the candidate will also give the recruiter more information about what the candidate is searching for in the new job. Based on this and on the rest of the interview, a pitch can be prepared to further sell the company to this candidate.

There are two things that must be done by the recruiter in order to generate a genuine interest.

Give a fair idea of the company's vision

A performance-driven employee is intelligent enough to evaluate the company's strategic decision and calculate its growth potential. They know that they will grow only if the company grows. If they gain confidence in the company's vision, they can see themselves being a part of a successful future.

At the root of most decisions is a simple question—"What's in it for me?".

We are positive towards something only when there is something in it for us. The candidate is not wrong to think along similar lines, because that's where the motivation to perform is derived from. It could be money, power, recognition, learning, or many other things contributing to an employee's professional and personal development. Tell the candidate how important their department, their role, and their personal and team contribution would be for the management, and in what manner this contribution is recognized and rewarded in your company.

Future prospects and career development opportunities

An employee with a long-term vision and career goal is always lured by a job that offers more than money—a job that looks after the candidate's all-encompassing career development. A recruiter must be able to describe the training initiatives and the career growth opportunities an employee may expect from their organization. Today, most companies prefer their own performers to fill strategic leadership positions. Lateral hiring is done only when no such person is available within the system. Give the candidates something special to look forward to that only you have, a **Unique Selling Point**, enticing enough for an industry performer.

Besides this, the candidate must also be informed about other things such as leave policies, work-life balance priorities, typical work environment, and anything else that the candidate might not bring up but that could be vital to their final decision and performance later on.

So far, we have constructed the path that a successful telephone recruiter must follow, but just like every other process, there are certain areas on this route that must be avoided. Putting it simply, there are certain mistakes that must be avoided during a telephone interview to ensure its success. Move on to the next chapter to learn what they are.

Summary

Planning is the key element that leads to a successful telephone interview, and must be done at both macro as well as micro level. Macro-planning helps in identifying the underlying cause behind the hiring, its requirements, and expectations from the candidate, whereas micro-planning helps organize the interview in a meticulous manner.

Broadly categorized into five segments, a well-defined assortment of open-ended questions contributes constructively to the telephone interview. The questions must also be adapted into real-life situations demanding impromptu answers from the candidate to check the authenticity of their answers.

A candidate's answers must be recorded and categorically evaluated, creating a formative assessment for the candidate. Detailed discussion and assessment of the facts including education records, profile relevance, industry and business knowledge, personality traits, and behavior patterns is extremely important and must be properly documented and analyzed.

Selling the job can be initiated by the interviewer inviting the candidate to ask questions. The interviewer must identify key selling points that are relevant to the candidate, which can later be used to close the deal. Moreover, the interviewer must take the opportunity to effectively communicate about the company and its vision, the role and its contribution, and finally, the career opportunities the company may have in store for a top-performing candidate.

In the next chapter, I have listed all the mistakes that even the best trained and most experienced recruiters tend to make, along with the potential damages that may be caused by making them. Read on and learn to avoid making those errors yourself.

>4

Avoid Common Mistakes

To persuade a candidate to join a vacant position, a mutual desire for association must be generated through a series of discussions. That means both parties are simultaneously buying and selling; the interviewer's decision to hire and the interviewee's decision to join are equally significant. The success of an interview process, especially when it's conducted via telephone, is largely contingent upon the interviewer's performance. As we discussed in previous chapters, there are many things that an interviewer must do to reach a conclusive decision. But an interviewer should be equally careful about the things that they must not do to ensure that the candidate does not come away with a negative opinion about the interviewer, job, or the company.

I have always believed throughout my recruitment career that in interviews, sometimes doing what one shouldn't has had a greater impact impact than not doing what one should have done. This chapter elaborates upon what an interviewer should not do: the common mistakes that should be avoided in any telephone interview.

The errors discussed in this chapter may be made at various stages of the telephone-interview process, and each error comes with its own bundle of ramifications that are always negative and often irreparable. Mistakes are principally the result of carelessness or lack of seriousness.

The first and foremost mistake that an interviewer can make is to treat telephone interviews casually. After reading the first three chapters, I am sure that we all must have reached the conclusion that a telephone interview can play a unique role in saving time, effort, and cost, while enhancing the productivity and efficiency of the entire hiring process. Once you start believing that the process is insignificant, mistakes creep in at almost every stage. The interviewer must begin by taking the process seriously.

The pressure to hire is another big factor that leads to mistakes. The longer a position remains vacant, the higher the pressure to fill it. Naturally, this increases the recruiter's stress, leading to hasty decision making and compromised candidate quality. Always remember that the consequences of a bad hire are more calamitous than the opportunity cost of a vacant position.

Now, assuming that we are all on the same page in terms of the effort we wish to put into making ourselves better telephone interviewers, let's identify, discuss, and find ways to eliminate the various mistakes made at each phase of the interview process.

Planning phase

If you don't take it seriously, you simply won't plan for it. Failure to plan properly and with due care is the single greatest pitfall into which interviewers fall and is at the heart of most other errors. To make it more specific, listed in the following sections are some very common mistakes that must be avoided at all costs.

One-sided scheduling of interviews

In the hope of fixing things up faster, interviewers make blunders such as calling up without notice, being late, unapologetically cancelling the call, or inviting more interviewers than the candidate was informed about; this can make the whole experience unpleasant for the candidate.

Not analyzing and defining the requirement

Unless a recruiter analyzes the key characteristics of the requirement and clearly defines the traits to look for in a candidate, they are liable to make mistakes in the interview. If the interviewer isn't aware of the specific skills and attributes required, how can they ask the right questions? Or how can they correctly analyze the answers once they get them? But if the macro-planning is carefully done as suggested in *Chapter 3, Plan, Conduct, and Assess*, of this book, the recruiter will feel highly prepared and confident before dialing the numbers of the prospective candidates, and it will make all the difference to the outcome.

Unstructured interview

Either due to hiring pressure, lack of time, or simply out of ignorance, many recruiters often don't feel the need to lay out a proper interview design or structure. Unfortunately, unlike a face-to-face interview, on the telephone, it won't be possible to recover from this mistake. Hence, once the requirement analysis is carefully chalked out, a recruiter should spend a few minutes preparing a list of questions to be asked. They should also be aware of the kind of answers they should be expecting from the ideal candidate and the key characteristics specially needed for the role at hand.

We want the candidates to feel sincere about the telephone interview. This means we must take it seriously ourselves and thus set the tone. The only way to do that is to plan thoroughly. Planning is always evident when it has been done, and can be felt over the phone as well from the confidence in your voice and the flow and logical coherence of questions. A fumbling and chaotic recruiter hints at the initial stage of the interview that they have not planned, giving the impression that the candidate need not worry about the interview as it appears to only be an ice-breaker.

Communication errors

Before we move on to identifying missteps at more technical and advanced stages of the telephone interview, first we must check our communication strategy, because after planning, communication is the second most important deciding factor behind the success or failure of a telephone interview. Listed as follows are some errors to avoid.

Ambiguous role descriptions

Communication with the candidate commences when the role description is sent to them, and that's where many recruiters make a mistake. General responsibilities are usually listed in bullets, but specifics are not mentioned. For example, the role description of a general sales profile mentions that the candidate will be expected to manage customer services as well, but it is seldom mentioned as to what extent the role involves customer services. This leads to confusion and suspicion about the role in the candidate's mind.

The following diagram consists of two role descriptions of the same profile—general and detailed. The candidate who got the general description may not be able to understand the role completely and might go ahead with the interview just for the sake of exploration. However, once they get to understand the role completely during the interview, they may not find it interesting enough and could end up refusing to move ahead. The candidate cannot be blamed for this as they were not given a clear idea of the role at an earlier stage. On the other hand, the candidate who got the detailed role description as given in the following diagram will have an unambiguous perception of the role and the extent of various responsibilities that he or she might have to handle. So, the decision of going ahead with the interview will be more conscious and rational, further enhancing the chances of a successful hire.

Role Descriptions For 'Area Manager Sales'

Key Rresponsibility Areas (KRAs)

> Managing the sales of Financial Services Products in the assigned area
> Achieving the sales targets
> Team Management
> Handling cutomer services

<———— General

Detailed ————>

Key Responbsibility Areas (KRAs)

Sales:

> Manage sales targets of Financial Products Services in unsecured loans business
> Cross-selling of investment products like insurance, D-mat accounts, and savings accounts
>Achieve monthly sales targets
> Leads generation through cold calling and tele calling

Team Management:

> No direct reportees, but coordinating with credits and operations teams
> Managing two process executives for quick processing of application forms

Customer Services:

> Relationship management with existing customers
> Guiding them to the relevant departments as per their requirements
> Managing their financial portfolios
> Other services like payment reminders etc.

Not making the candidate comfortable

This is an interview and not an interrogation, and this difference must be clearly understood by the recruiter. If we want our candidate to talk openly to us, we must make them comfortable with the warmth of our conversation. This can be done by keeping a smile in your voice, laughing, and using positive expressions to put them at ease. Little things can make a difference. Rephrasing a routine icebreaker such as "You sent your resume for this opening yesterday" into a more positive "We have quite an interesting opening for a candidate just like you" will make a candidate feel praised, important, and desired. Intimidating the candidate will never achieve any results. The interviewer is supposed to create a friendly conversational environment over the phone. Smile with a warm greeting. If you think it doesn't matter and are doubtful as to whether the candidate can really feel it or not, try saying hello to someone you know over the phone—once with a smile and once without it—and ask if they feel a difference. They will.

Making the interview a monologue

Remember, in an interview, 95 percent of the speaking opportunity should go to the candidate and the other 5 percent to the recruiter. Usually, this is far from the reality. A good interviewer is a good listener. Although talking more may make the recruiter feel better, and more in control of the whole conversation, in the end, in order to effectively assess a candidate, you must give them a chance to speak at length.

Using local slang, idioms, or dialect

We have already discussed how organizations are becoming global in their hiring initiatives. Now, if you are hiring a brilliant software brain from, let's say, China, using local slang or phrases in your conversation could jeopardize the whole effort. A person in another part of the world is equipped to understand formal English, but is not ready to understand local slang. Using slang will not leave the candidate with a positive impression. There is also a risk that you will prejudice your own assessment of the candidate based on their perceived inability to communicate effectively, ignoring the fact that to create best-selling software, they must be good in the technology that creates the software, not at local conversational slang.

Interview phase

We must have realized and noted by now that the lack of planning is the mother of all mistakes. Every other failure down the line, fundamentally comes back to a lack of planning, and its ramifications can be impossible to predict. During the interview itself, planning ahead—even just by reading this book—will help you avoid specific mistakes that cause particular kinds of damage. We will explore some common errors to look out for when assessing your own telephone interview process in the following sections.

Testing knowledge and not action

Ask a candidate "How should your relationship be with your boss?" and you'll get a lot of information regurgitated from the Internet while learning nothing about the candidate except that they have taken the time to Google. However, if you ask "Please recall a situation when you believed that your boss was doing something incorrectly. How did you communicate it to them and how did you handle the situation?", you'll get a much better result. Candidates can't foresee such questions, so the answers cannot be rehearsed in advance. The candidate will have no option but to narrate a true incident, and no matter how much the candidate tries to manipulate it, if something negative had happened, you'll hear it in their voice or through verbal clues. It's difficult to manipulate the facts in an impromptu answer.

Not digging deep enough

Having asked the question given previously, most recruiters leave the issue with the answer provided by the candidate and make a judgment based on that. A trained recruiter will dig deeper. They will ask all sorts of consequential questions, such as what happened? Why did it happen? Why do you think your boss was wrong; could you have been mistaken in how you perceived the situation? The discussion can be drawn out until the recruiter is actually satisfied that the course of action and behavior demonstrated by the candidate was justified and ideal for the given situation, proving the candidate's good sense of judgment and ability to handle relationships well at work.

Trying to dodge the interviewee's queries

Another mistake that most recruiters make is in not welcoming the candidate's queries. Either their questions are never invited, or they are dodged until the face-to-face interview, or they are not supplied with a candid answer. A seasoned recruiter always wants their candidate to have a fair chance to ask questions about the role, job, and the company, as they understand there is value behind this exercise in terms of establishing the candidate's interest and trust.

Trying to make a mental note of most of the information

All I have to say is this: *it is not possible*. Without making proper notes or using an appropriate recording system, you may remember some information out of a 30-45 minute discussion with the candidate, but most of it, I assure you, will be lost. Notes save you from forming judgments based on a half-cooked assessment. Additionally, if the other recruiters get a copy of such notes, it helps the entire recruiting team to form a collective judgment based on all the notes accumulated, preventing any kind of bias resulting from one person's judgment.

Assessment phase

Mistakes made at the previous stages still stand a chance of rectification and pose a less severe threat to the outcome of the interview, but the ones made at this stage are the ugliest and come with damages that are not only beyond repair, but that could also cause ripple effects.

Intuition-based assessment

Well, what else can you do except go with your intuition or gut-feeling if you haven't got a formal system for assessing candidates based on analysis of the job requirements? But just as a quick reminder—remember the cost of a bad hire. Gut-feeling is usually not a handy tool when it comes to judging someone. Try to recall the last electronics purchase you made. How many questions did you ask about performance, wattage, customer service, warranty, and so on? And here we are talking about only a few hundred dollars. So imagine the cautiousness you need when selecting a person who has their own mind and is a huge investment of your resources. Adopt formal assessment systems by making proper notes and documents that can be analyzed after the interview to make a proper assessment!

Stuck in the Tolstoy Trap

Remember Eggers and Leary's "Tolstoy Trap", which we covered in *Chapter 3, Plan, Conduct, and Assess*? Though they have used it in a different context, I believe that it applies broadly to basic human psychology. They stated that "we always tend to see what we already believe in." We all must have experienced this at least once in our lives. I longed for a car once which was not, in fact, a very popular model. I kept seeing it in abundance on roads just because I liked it and I wanted to believe that it was good and popular, even if it wasn't. Trust me, the day I decided to buy it, I was *sure* I saw every fifth person on the road driving the same car. We, as human beings, tend to be prejudiced towards our preconceived notions, and this gets translated into our decisions. Don't let yourself fall into this Tolstoy Trap. The choice of car didn't hurt me much; however, hiring a bad candidate or losing a good one surely would. If we start the interview with preconceived notions, there is a strong possibility that we will only observe the points we were searching for and will ignore the additional important ideas contributed by the candidate, which could be extremely important for our company's business.

Using the wrong benchmarks for comparison

This is a further extension of our unconscious biases. We talked to a candidate and we liked their answers. Now, the general tendency is that when we speak to another candidate, we use the previous candidate's answers as a yardstick. Yet ideally, we should evaluate each candidate's responses in light of the role requirements alone.

I have said this many times earlier, but that won't prevent me from repeating it again: it is essential that assessment should always be formalized, ongoing, targeted, analytical, and based on the notes and facts accumulated.

The job selling phase

Competition amongst companies for getting the best people and the apprehension of candidates for perceived job security has triggered a phase in which the recruiter, at the final stage of the interview, has to act like a salesman, pitching their job offer as well as the company in a convincing manner. But while doing so, a recruiter must remember the limitations and refrain from being carried away. Correct information is crucial to a candidate.

The pressure to hire the best person within the strictest possible deadline is so high that recruiters often tend to miss-sell or over-sell, both of which are extremely detrimental to the future employee's relationships, as well as the organization's brand image in the employment market.

While miss-selling means giving incorrect facts (often more colorful than they actually are) about the job and the organizational policies, over-selling refers to creating incorrect **expectations** for the candidates related to the **opportunities** the job may offer or the project a candidate may be assigned. For example, offering the candidate a customer services role while actually the job involves selling is an example of miss-selling, whereas selling the opportunity of team-leading based on performance, which could never be achieved before a minimum tenure of two years as per the company policy, is an over-sell.

To you this may just seem like adding a touch of polish, but from the perspective of the candidate, it's simply a fraudulent practice which they will never approve of, no matter how hard you try to justify it later. If the candidate is well connected, they will learn the truth before making any decision, and could do a great deal of damage in the market for your organization's brand image.

Make a note

Sometimes, choosing the right words makes all the difference. The recruiter should only provide information that is confirmed and accurate. The candidate has a tendency to translate possible into confirmed. So, if you tell them that there is a possibility of a new project on which they could learn a new technology, the candidate usually takes it as confirmed and makes their decision accordingly. But what if the deal doesn't come through? The candidate, who is an employee now, will feel cheated and be less productive. They may even start looking out for other opportunities. So, it's imperative for the recruiter to speak only about the things that are confirmed and that are not simply a possibility.

All the errors listed at different stages in this chapter may seem to be very elementary or something that we are already aware of, but it's that very attitude that leads us to make one or more of them with alarming frequency. And that's where I started this chapter from—attitude. Bring out a positive change in your attitude and you will automatically eliminate a lot of errors.

Summary

Attitude is the key culprit behind all our failures and mistakes in the hiring process. Everything else is just a chain of outcomes—one leading to another. So, the principal mistake is a casual attitude towards the whole process. Once a recruiter understands and believes in the potential benefits derived from a sound telephone-interview system, a bucket full of problems will evaporate.

Errors in judgment can happen at any stage of the interview. Process errors can be rectified by adequate planning and keen observation with repeated required adjustments, but psychological errors like prejudiced judgment are fatal to the process. Formalization of the process is the key to stamping out psychological barriers to change.

Both miss-selling and over-selling can be detrimental to the career of the arriving candidate. To settle down and become productive in a new organization, the candidate needs reassurance that whatever was promised to them—that they believed—is true and possible, given their performance. When the picture turns out to be false or vastly different, such trust gets shattered, and that can create negative waves for the company across the industry. In the final chapter, you will learn the various ways in which the art of conducting a telephone interview can be practiced, evaluated, and mastered. You will also observe that top management's interest is extremely important if company-wide training has to be initiated. Finally, you will be provided with certain tools that are essential for assessment and improvement.

>5

Master the Skill – Training and Development

Now that you've learned the massive benefits to be gained from good telephone interviews (and the detrimental effects when the process is poorly designed or badly conducted), let's finish with some advice on how to implement best-practice telephone interviewing strategies in your company.

Developing any management skill, including conducting telephone interviews, requires **initiative, mentoring,** and **evaluation**. In this case, it will probably fall to the Human Resources department to assume the roles of an initiator, promoter, and coach. The onus of a bad hire or the credit of a good hire belongs to the HR department. At the same time, no management will ever approve of a new process, especially in such tumultuous times, unless it's proven worthwhile. In this case, the training initiative is aimed at training team leaders, which will cost valuable man hours. So, it is HR's responsibility to convince management of the potential tangible and intangible benefits and champion the idea of internal coaching and evaluation for team leaders. The benefits are real and simple: once the leaders are sensitized towards the dynamics of a phone screen that are different from those of a face-to-face interview and are adequately trained in conducting a telephone interview, interviewing will be vastly more successful.

The following chart illustrates the process of experimentation, which begins with the trained recruiters practicing the telephone-interview process under the guidance of the HR department head.

The head of HR then evaluates and presents the results to the management in order to promote company-wide training in the process, and aid in developing the skill throughout the leadership by regular practice and evaluation.

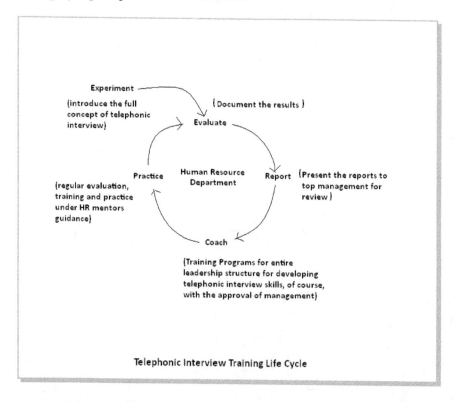

Telephonic Interview Training Life Cycle

There are two elementary steps towards gaining an expertise in this vital business skill: classroom training and implementation.

Classroom training

Organize classroom training programs that focus on orientation towards developing the skill by sharing the results of the experiment, management, and organizational interest, and finally laying out the plan of action by providing a comparative analysis of the current methods and the new model. This should be followed by a live demonstration by an HR/recruitment expert or a recording of the same, wherein two candidates are interviewed—one with the conventional method and the other using your proposed telephone interview method. Training delivers best results when the proposed action is demonstrated "live". During demonstration, all the forms that were suggested during this entire book should be used so that people can relate to the efficiency and productivity of the telephone-interview process and can realize the results it can deliver if implemented properly.

Implementation

One can become a competent telephone interviewer only by doing it. It would be highly impractical to think that every hiring leader could be accompanied by a recruitment mentor during a telephone interview to evaluate the interview performance. It can only be done if the telephone interviewers are able to evaluate themselves using prescribed forms and standard procedures. On the other hand, how could the HR department, without being involved, collect performance-related data for further analysis and presentation? Two activities are needed to be able to regularly monitor whether the training has been implemented in a result-oriented manner:

1. Appraise each telephone interview session formally. You can use the following template to do so:

Telephonic Interview - Interviewer's Interview Session Appraisal Checklist

Candidate's Name: _____   Date and Time for Interview: _____

Position Considered For: _____   Interviewer: _____

Department: _____   Interview Duration _____

Checklist	Yes	No
1. Did I plan as per the 'Planning Checklist and Planning Form'?		
2. Could I establish the purpose of the interview and was clear about the requirement and related expectations?		
3. Did I start the conversation warmly and make the candidate comfortable?		
4. Did I ask more open-ended questions. relevant to the job opening?		
5. Was I a good listener, as per the 'Telephonic Interview Listening Skills Assessment Checklist?		
6. Did I ask questions from different categories to ensure that I could catch any contradictions or false statement?		
7. Did I record the conversation as specified?		
8. Did I make notes as per the 'Candidate Assessment Sheet'?		
9. Could I sell the job effectively as guided without over-selling or miss-selling?		
10. Were my questions based on testing the action and not knowledge?		
11. Do I feel that my evaluation of the candidate is based on my notes and not on a prejudiced notion?		

A 99.9% success rate may be assured if the answers to all the above questions stand 'Yes'.

Training Initiative Feedback (Additional)

1. Did the 'Formal' training in 'Telephonic Interview Skills' enhanced the quality of interview?
2. Was planning, scheduling and assessment based on the forms, sheets and checklists effective?
3. Do I see an improvement in my telephonic conversation mannerisms, especially listening skills?
4. Do I believe that effective telephonic inteview saved a great deal of my time and stress?
5. Could I assess the candidate more objectively that I believe would enhance the quality of the the incoming employee?

Additionally, if the answers to the questions above are 'Yes'
It will tell the HR mentors about the effectiveness of the Training Program and help in determining the future course of action.

---

2. Analyze the training needs of the interviewer using the following template:

Telephonic Interview Skills - Interviewer's Training Need Analysis Form

Assessment Date: _____   Interviewer's Name: _____

Sample Size: _____   HR Mentor's Name: _____

(Number of Interview Sessions used)

Issues Resolved Post Training	Persistent Problems	Regularly Recurring Concerns

Subsequent Training and Discussion Required

Problem 1	Problem 2	Problem 3

This form would enable the mentors to correctly identify the problems hiring leaders may be facing, evaluate the reasons, prioritize the ones that need immediate action and find a solution by spotting further training needs.

Make a note

The first activity must be carried out by the telephone interviewers after every telephone interview they conduct. The second is the responsibility of the telephone recruitment mentors or the trained human resource professionals.

An evaluation of each telephone interview session principally serves two purposes. First and foremost, it enables the recruiter to identify the notable changes that have resulted due to the prioritization and formalization of the telephone interview process. Moreover, it also serves as documentary evidence of the things that were either accomplished or missed during the process. It also highlights areas of improvement.

Secondly, it creates a stream of **valuable data** that can be used by the HR department for further analysis to improve the skills of the individual recruiter.

A training-needs analysis must be done on a sample of 10-15 telephone interview sessions per interviewer. Using a sample is important for:

> ➤ Ensuring that the interviewer is employing the new improved system regularly
> ➤ Identifying the changes due to formal implementation of the process
> ➤ Observing the improvements in the recruitment process and productivity
> ➤ Spotting any regular problem that the interviewer might be facing and that needs immediate attention and training

Periodical training needs analyses will ensure that accumulated data can be analyzed and results can be drawn and presented to the management. Moreover, it will also alert the HR team if something with the process as a whole or any individual recruiter goes wrong and will push them to take remedial action without losing the most valuable commodity: time.

Across the book, I have used the word "formal" profusely. The simple justification comes from the fact that unless a management practice, including the telephone interview, is introduced "formally"—that is to say that unless the executive board senses the value behind it—getting approval for the investment needed in terms of time and resources won't be easy. Besides, if the executive board is not interested enough to implement it, one cannot expect the team leaders to accept it wholeheartedly. Hence, the first step, again at the cost of repeating myself, is to change the attitude right from the top.

Summary

This book has clearly established the telephone interview as a strong solution to the current hiring problems that most global organizations are facing. Telephone interviews also solve the problem of searching for talented employees by enabling the recruiter to select candidates from a global pool while keeping the cost down.

This book has forced you to scrutinize the telephone-interview process you are currently following. Benchmarking against the right way to conduct a telephone interview made you aware of the errors that you may have been making currently.

You have learned that best results can be achieved through understanding the telephone-interview process in great detail. Once you understand the nuances involved with the telephone-interview process, it will be easier for you to properly plan and conduct the interviews. Proper planning will also enable you to create formal assessment procedures that will lead to better outcomes.

Additionally, the book also provides a comprehensive stage-wise list of the common mistakes that interviewers make while conducting a telephone interview. These mistakes can lead to severe damage for organizations, so such mistakes should be avoided at all cost. Refer back to our examples regularly to make sure you don't fall into common bad habits

Training in this area, like others, is a chain process that needs experimentation followed by management reporting and approval based on the data collected and analyzed. With management support, a formal training program can be initiated throughout the company with regular monitoring and evaluation.

Perhaps the most important lesson to take away from this book is that it is our attitudes that need to be tailored first in order to understand the need and importance of developing this skill as a company-wide initiative. Unless the telephone interview is taken seriously as an important process worthy of time, effort, and formal training, its massive potential benefits will be lost. And unless the top management backs up the plans, the leadership ladder won't take it up earnestly and the whole gamut of efforts will eventually fail; so, take the time to do things properly.

If you follow all the directions and advice given in this book, you will be well on your way to conducting successful and effective telephone interviews.